Little Laureates

Verses From Cumbria
Edited by Donna Samworth

Young Writers

First published in Great Britain in 2007 by:
Young Writers
Remus House
Coltsfoot Drive
Peterborough
PE2 9JX
Telephone: 01733 890066
Website: www.youngwriters.co.uk

SB ISBN 978-1 84602 984 4

Foreword

Young Writers was established in 1991 and has been passionately devoted to the promotion of reading and writing in children and young adults ever since. The quest continues today. Young Writers remains as committed to the nurturing of poetic and literary talent as ever.

This year's Young Writers competition has proven as vibrant and dynamic as ever and we are delighted to present a showcase of the best poetry from across the UK and in some cases overseas. Each poem has been selected from a wealth of *Little Laureates* entries before ultimately being published in this, our sixteenth primary school poetry series.

Once again, we have been supremely impressed by the overall quality of the entries we have received. The imagination, energy and creativity which has gone into each young writer's entry made choosing the poems a challenging and often difficult but ultimately hugely rewarding task - the general high standard of the work submitted ensured this opportunity to bring their poetry to a larger appreciative audience.

We sincerely hope you are pleased with this final collection and that you will enjoy *Little Laureates Verses From Cumbria* for many years to come.

Contents

John Colwell (8)   39
Ailsa Duncan (7)   40
William Ferdinand (7)   41
Isabella Harrison (7)   42
Thomas Harrison (8)   43
Jane Irving (7)   44
Isabel Leitch (7)   45
Joseph Logue (8)   46
Bruce Long (8)   47
Daniel Lumb (8)   48
Rory Sutton (8)   49
Christian Wood (7)   50
Adrian Anderson (7)   51
Harry Blowing (8)   52
Georgina Clough (7)   53
Oskar Nicholson (8)   54
Kathryn Orr (8)   55
Molly Pattinson (7)   56
May Percival (7)   57
Rupert Rosindell (8)   58
Ellie Routledge (7)   59
Martin Wright (8)   60
Gemma Stacey (10)   61

Gosforth CE Primary School
Melissa Chesterman (9)   62
Adam Aldridge (10)   63
William Hughes (10)   64
Joe Barker (9)   65
Joseph Smith (9)   66
Scott Vandepeear (10)   67
Lauren Dawson (10)   68
Dani Lewis (9)   69
Sam Farrar (10)   70
Kathleen Coverley Naylor (10)   71
Georgia Clarke (9)   72
Grant Mounsey (11)   73
Kate Mitchell (9)   74
Callum Atkinson (10)   75
Andrew Hilton (11)   76
Erin Marley (11)   77

Allard Newell (10)	78
Pepijn van den Elzen (9)	79

Greengate Junior School

Bethany Murray (10)	80
Debeny McPoland (10)	81
Danielle Hardman (11)	82
Jay Cresswell (10)	83
Sam Loughran (10)	84
Sam Pickering (11)	85
David Morgan (10)	86
Chloe Smith (10)	87
Lauren Purcell (11)	88
Jason Caine (11)	89
Ryan Sharkey (11)	90
Connor Reid (10)	91
Steven Logan (11)	92
Liam Pollard (10)	93
Morgan Bowes (10)	94
Jordan Kenrick (10)	95
Rebekka Heslop (10)	96
Hayley Williams (10)	97
Abby Readhead (10)	98
Abigail Hardie (10)	99
Jemma Young (11)	100
Chantelle Mayor (11)	101
Jodie Leonard (11)	102
Jesse Powell (10)	103
Nathan Jasper (11)	104
Nikki Weall (10)	105
Vanessa Graham (10)	106
Cathy Rawlings (10)	107
Lauren Edwards (11)	108
Sam Crawford (11)	109
Kimberley Sayle (11)	110
Chloe Hilton (10)	111
Michaela Halliday (11)	112
Matthew Lightfoot (10)	113
Nia Studt (10)	114
Brandon Edmondson (10)	115
Irene Courtney (11)	116

Hunter Hall School

Becky Hurst (9)   156
Isabella Sharrock (8)   157
Julia Addison (7)   158
Louisa Evans (7)   159
Fintan Simmons (7)   160
Connie Hurton (7)   161
Saskia Rockliffe-King (8)   162
Sophina Boyd (8)   163
Paige-Olivia Lee (7)   164
James Carruthers (8)   165
Alice Addison (7)   166
Nicholas Sowerby (7)   167
Georgia Birley (10)   168
Brook Birley (9)   169
India Birley (7)   170

Kirkoswald CE Primary School
Anya Wilcock (10)   171
Ian Oliver (9)   172
Dan Todd (9)   173
Katrina Blenkharn (9)   174
Callum Latimer (11)   175
Hannah Frost (10)   176
Ellie Armstrong (10)   177
Calum Lennie (10)   178
Sam Borgogno (11)   179
Connie Dalton (10)   180

Robert Ferguson Primary School
Lydia McGuiness (9)   181
Joshua Allen (8)   182
Naomi Evans (8)   183
Alice McLean (9)   184
Ebony Harper (9)   185
Becky Ward (8)   186
Courtney Wood (8)   187
Jade Selen (9)   188
Thomas Chandler (9)   189
Kelly Pearson (8)   190
Amy Stobbart (8)   191
Luke Green (8)   192

The Poems

My Pet Rozsi

My dog Rozsi can get very dozy.
She always wants to play during the day.
She plays with my cat and toy bat.
She is medium-sized with big round eyes that glisten in the sun.
When she goes to the park all she does is bark.
She has loads of friends; they always drive me round the bend!
At night she goes to sleep, she doesn't even make a peep!

Lizzie Colwell (10)
Austin Friars St Monica's School

My Quad Bike

My quad bike is red
The seat is as comfy as a bed
Its size is a 400cc
My dad says it suits me.

My quad bike goes so fast
It never comes last
It whizzes down the field in fifth gear
And comes back in a drift.

My quad bike always needs a clean
So it looks very mean
I like to ride it everywhere
When I am on it I have no care.

Nicky Dixon (11)
Austin Friars St Monica's School

A Journey Of Books

Wouldn't it be funny if books could speak?
They'd talk about journeys to a dangerous peak,
An exciting pilgrimage, adventures galore,
Mutinies, murders and much, much more!
Wouldn't it be funny if books could talk
About a playful blue dolphin and a flying brown hawk,
About fierce lions on the African plains,
And black and white pandas eating bamboo canes.
Books have lots of different stories
About huge defeats and incredible glories.
About witches and wizards waving their wands,
About clever spies and young James Bonds.
Books are honest, true and don't lie,
They go deep underwater and high in the sky.
You're probably thinking, *could this happen to me?*
Well go get a book, just wait and we'll see!

Loren Ewart (10)
Austin Friars St Monica's School

My Cat Posh

Posh has green eyes like some ripe grapes about to fall.
She always likes to play with her cat scratcher and her ball.
She has a brown mark on her face that looks like a coffee stain.
When Posh has a wash she always sounds like she's in pain.

Posh has four little white feet like she's walked in some snow.
When she is about to pounce she crouches down low.
Posh sleeps by my feet on the soft pink throw
And sometimes plays with my bright pink toe.

She can climb up trees right to the top
And she lets her tail hang low and flop.
Her tail is brown with a hint of white
But she never gets into a fight.

Portia Inglis (11)
Austin Friars St Monica's School

The Horse Ride

I glide swiftly across the bay
On a sunny hot summer's day.
The field around me, a fuzzy blur,
Bobby's fine tail against brown fur.
I forget all around me, the birds and trees,
A wonderful feeling in my legs and knees.
My arms like jelly, my hands like lead.
Like an amazing dream in my warm cosy bed.
Bobby's hooves make a rhythm on the ground,
Almost a song, a sweet and nice sound.

Grace Jamieson (11)
Austin Friars St Monica's School

Bears

There are all sorts of bears,
Of all shapes and sizes.
They have thick soft fur
And big brown eyes.
Polar bears have lovely white fur
Grizzly bears are big and quite scary
Spectacled have colourful eyes
And brown bears are big and hairy!

Ellen Jardine (11)
Austin Friars St Monica's School

My Dog - Haiku

My dog comes and plays
My dog likes to fetch frisbees
My dog is cute too!

Jack Ling (10)
Austin Friars St Monica's School

My Favourite Holiday

When we go to Center Parcs
We live in a house in the wood,
There are lots of things to do there
So our holidays are always good!

We go out cycling
Along all the paths,
Even though it's quiet
Mum makes us wear safety hats.

You can have a go at fencing,
You learn sword fighting,
There's no physical contact
Especially no biting!

Dad and I go swimming
In the indoor pool,
He loses his trunks on the slide
And looks like a fool!

By the end of the day
When I go to bed,
I'm absolutely shattered
And have a bad head.

Robyn Nixon (11)
Austin Friars St Monica's School

Chewed Up Homework!

My dog chewed up my homework,
It really wasn't me,
I wish it wasn't English
And rather maths, dear me!

I brought my dog to school,
I really regret it now,
Because all my teachers said
Was to get the homework out!

Niamh Orr (10)
Austin Friars St Monica's School

My Friend Nicky - Haiku

My best friend Nicky
Likes to ride his quad all day
He enters races.

Tom Percival (10)
Austin Friars St Monica's School

Newcastle United Toon Fans - Haiku

The Newcastle fans
We are Sunderland haters
We beat them four-one.

Marcus Pieri (11)
Austin Friars St Monica's School

Newcastle United - Haiku

My favourite team
Their nickname is the 'Magpies'
They hate Sunderland.

Barnaby Robson (11)
Austin Friars St Monica's School

My Dog Had A Bed - Haiku

My dog had a bed
All fluffy and red and blue
And it was comfy.

Toby Robson (11)
Austin Friars St Monica's School

My Rabbit Freddy - Haiku

My rabbit Freddy
He loves to eat lots of food
And is very nice.

Max Routledge (10)
Austin Friars St Monica's School

Anger

It smells like ash.
It tastes like carrot soup.
It sounds like a lion.
It looks like a picture of nothing.
It feels like a bumpy rock.
It reminds me of fire.
It is anger.

Logan Davidson (9)
Austin Friars St Monica's School

Giggles

Oh no! they're back,
Popcorn popping in my head,
Candyfloss puffed up,
On a roller coaster, up and down,
Going round the bend,
Popcorn and candyfloss everywhere!
Pop! The giggles are back!

Sophie Ferdinand (9)
Austin Friars St Monica's School

Happiness

Happiness smells like roses.
Happiness sounds like running water.
Happiness tastes like favourite foods.
Happiness looks like food.

Joseph Harrison (9)
Austin Friars St Monica's School

Anger

Anger is like the smoke of death.
It is as loud as a volcano waiting in the shadows like a silent killer.
It is like the bitter taste of blood and an ancient creature waiting
to escape.
It is hiding in people and sometimes it leaps out!
It is as cold as frost in winter but as hot as lava flowing from a volcano.
It is as deep as the Pacific Ocean.

John Long (10)
Austin Friars St Monica's School

Anger

It's burning inside me again!
The anger is brewing up,
Burning like a bonfire from the depths of Hell!
It's like a volcano erupting
Steam gushing out of my ears
Lava pouring out of my mouth.

Joe Shadwick (9)
Austin Friars St Monica's School

Anger

I've got that feeling again,
She's given me that look.
She's stolen my PSP,
My body feels like thumping her but that won't help.
I feel like roaring just like a lion,
I can taste rusty nails in my mouth,
It seems like I'm looking at Hell.
It will go soon, I hope it will go soon.

George Sims (10)
Austin Friars St Monica's School

Anger

Anger boils up in my head,
It feels like smoke burning inside
Waiting to explode
Hot with hatred.
The lion's roar erupts,
My head feels detracted from my body.
It's over in an instant,
My rigid emotions have passed.

William Stonebridge (10)
Austin Friars St Monica's School

Bully Victim

Down in my heart I feel so sad
Yet on the outside I feel glad.
In my heart I can smell fear
Yet on the outside I smell fresh deer.

My heart makes me taste medicine
But my outside makes me taste an iced bun.
Inside I can hear a witch cackling at me crying
But on the outside I can hear myself laughing.

The picture on the inside is horrible and darkening
Yet on the outside I see flowers all blooming.
My heart feels broken and bad
On the outside though it feels bright and glad.

And the whole point of this is when being bullied
Tell someone and you won't feel worried.

Chloe Thomson (9)
Austin Friars St Monica's School

Sadness

S adness is not nice
A nd it feels like ice.
D ogs put their tails in-between their legs
N osy twits go as white as eggs
E mpty rooms feel just like it
S adness tastes like oranges and it
S ounds like a long goodbye.

Taran Vear (10)
Austin Friars St Monica's School

Hunger

Hunger is yellow
A yellow dog walks up the street
People eating yellow pancakes
People eating popcorn in a cinema
Painting pictures with yellow paint
People sitting down on a beach looking up at the sun.

Hunger is sweet
Squeezing juice out of a lemon
Pouring sugar into your mouth
Unwrapping a chocolate bar and then eating it
Drinking a hot cup of green tea
Dropping a sweet into your mouth.

Hunger is rough
Feeling dry grass
Scrunching up a piece of paper
Feeling cow skin
Using a blade of a sword
People holding big diamonds.

Hunger is a loud screech
A cat screeching and howling
Cars braking and then screeching
Watching a horror film at a scary bit
Somebody's chair screeching
A person sees a monster.

Hunger smells like food
People eating sushi
Burgers being made
Chips cooking in an oven
Shrimps being caught out at sea
Oats being ground to make bread.

Alastair Crippen (9)
Austin Friars St Monica's School

Unhappiness

Unhappiness is like standing in a graveyard alone,
You start to groan,
You're lonely; you're too scared to cry out
Because someone might put you in doubt.

It feels like ice, rough and cold,
It's like you're beginning to feel old.
You can't think about anything at all,
It feels like bashing into a wall.

It has no noise; it's quiet like in a quiet space.
You have a slow pace.
So alone in nothing but darkness,
You are in a very big mess.

It smells like rain,
Someone is in pain.
No one listens to you in your days of need,
Someone wants your money because of greed.

You can't see anything but black.
Black is so dark,
Black is loneliness,
Black is sadness.

James Main (9)
Austin Friars St Monica's School

Silence

It has no sound,
It's as strong as the ground.
It can feel as dark as night,
Which can give you a fright.

Silence is no fun,
It makes me want to scream and run.
Silence is nasty,
I won't let it catch me.

Silence is boring,
Enough to start snoring.
Silence is a daydream,
Do you know what I mean?

Silence has no colour,
It gets even duller.
Silence is like a crash,
It sounds like a smash.

When I come home all nice and dry,
I can't hear the sound of Jemima's cry.
Something's wrong, where are they?
My sixth sense is asking me,
Have they been out all day?

But here they come now, around the way,
Mum said they were in town all day.
So here is the end of my tale,
I hope it hasn't gone like a snail.

Haris Craig (10)
Austin Friars St Monica's School

Fun

Fun feels like chocolate that's hard
Tasty like some hard clay
It's bright and yellow
Like the bright sunset.

It sounds like a nice cool breeze
Smoothly flying past
It smells like fresh chips
With salt and vinegar.

It tastes like cakes
Different types of icing.
I can sense my friends
Having fun by the way they act.

Luke Ferguson (10)
Austin Friars St Monica's School

Fun

I like fun, as bright as the sun
It can be as white as paper
It's usually colourful like flags
But then come the scallywags!

It feels like a bright yellow
And also feels like the patterns of a cello
It is as bouncy as a ball
But when fun stops, the balls fall.

Fun sounds like a historical joke
With all the fun in it
But all the fun starts
To feel like a soap.

Fun smells like the golden smell of chips
But then you get hit by a whip.
I like the golden smell
But I don't like the sound of the whips.

It tastes like sweets
With lots of treats
But fun goes through the weeks
But sometimes it can taste like wheat.

Duncan Hill (10)
Austin Friars St Monica's School

Fun

Gooey ooey sweets, chewy and nice,
Gingerbread men with sugar and spice.
We are going to the beach for the day,
It is very, very sunny in May.
Running around, having lots of fun,
I really enjoy a nice sticky bun.

Fun on your birthday, having a big cake,
Or crispy golden chips freshly baked.
Playing with your dog or your cat,
Going to a magic show, see a rabbit out of a hat.
Eating an apple, crunchy and red,
Having a lie in, in your bed.

Fun is like having a brush through your hair,
Or crunching through a nice juicy pear.
Wearing a pair of brand new shoes,
A big chocolate bar just for you.
Jumping a skipping rope up and down,
A cute little puppy giving you a frown.

These are all the ways to have fun
If you have taken them all in, you have won.
Always remember to do it right,
Never ever get into a fight.
Now it is time to say goodbye,
To have lots of fun and never tell a lie.

Sarah Hughes (9)
Austin Friars St Monica's School

Loneliness

Loneliness fills me with darkness,
A strange horrible crying inside,
A black little dot in my heart,
A life without friendship and love.

I can see a black alleyway before me.
An old man without a wife,
A girl without any friends
And a horse riding to nowhere.

I hear moaning and groaning,
The cry of a baby abandoned,
A man about to die,
A never-ending screeching.

I smell a wall newly painted,
A heap of clothes not washed for weeks,
A baby's nappy
And a bottle of insecticide.

I feel a moth-eaten dress on my skin,
A smooth and never-ending space,
A static feeling of a balloon
And empty air.

I taste the bitter taste of raw onions
And salty tears.
A drop of blood
And water by itself.

But loneliness still creeps up on me
Creeps, creeps up on me!

Asha Nicholson (10)
Austin Friars St Monica's School

Silence

Silence is as cold as ice,
Silence is as tasty as water,
Silence is as black as the night sky,
Silence is as quiet as a mouse.

Silence is as scented as plain air
And silence is peaceful.
It is a way of thinking,
Silence is a strange feeling.

Silence is like walking which is unpleasant,
It is a feeling of loneliness and quiet.
Silence is a way of relaxing,
Silence can be scary with nobody around.

Silence can help you concentrate,
Silence can be a real help,
It can help by helping you think
And it cannot help by sometimes being very scary.

Robert Johnson (10)
Austin Friars St Monica's School

Fun

Fun is as bouncy as a ball,
Fun is as bright yellow as the sun,
Fun is as nice as chips,
Fun sounds like happiness,
Fun is as sweet as chocolate.

Fun shines like the sun,
Just like my mum.
It is brighter than any star,
Well, that is what I think so far.

Fun smells like a sweet chocolate cake with cream,
Fun looks like a fresh summer dream.
Fun feels like a smooth dolphin,
Fun tastes like chips in tomato sauce.

Fun shines like the stars,
Fun has no bars,
Fun is like playing football,
Fun is *great!*

Fun is like a cup of warm tea
On a cold, frosty morning.
It is as much fun as the sea,
It doesn't have a warning.

Alexander Watson (10)
Austin Friars St Monica's School

Happiness

Happiness to me is something you can see,
A smile that lasts a while.
Happiness is a feeling inside,
It keeps me warm like fluffy slippers.
Happiness lifts me up,
It's like bouncing on a bouncy castle.
Happiness is a lovely smell of flowers that have been picked for me,
Underneath a big oak tree.
Happiness is singing and laughing joyfully.

Happiness is my family and friends,
My pet dog, red and going to bed.
Happiness is thinking happy thoughts that come inside my head
Like strawberries and whipped cream,
That was a nice dream!
If you look into my eyes, you'll get a nice surprise
Because happiness is there in me.

Ellie Fisher (10)
Austin Friars St Monica's School

Chelsea

C helsea are champions
H ero in goals
E ngland is the country
L iving to win
S tadium, Stamford Bridge
E ager to win the League
A lways beat every team.

Charlie Graham (8)
Austin Friars St Monica's School

My Pony Fudge

M y pony Fudge is very nice
Y aps here and there, everywhere

P ops up and down on the jumps
O n Thursday night all the time
N ine till five, running like a clown!
Y es, she is definitely mad

F rightening when you ride her
U nderstands when you have treats for her
D oesn't have very good manners
G ets into the way a lot
E ating lots and having fun.

Tara Houston (9)
Austin Friars St Monica's School

Christmas

I love Christmas, it's so good.
I really love the Christmas pud.
I get presents and feel so glad
But when there's no Christmas I feel sad.
I feel happy when I do the tree
I got a scarf and it suits me!

Hannah Le Brocq (9)
Austin Friars St Monica's School

Ferrari

F erraris are first to the finish line
E very race counts
R ace cars
R evving engines
A ll Ferraris go so fast
R acing round and round the track
 I n every race, Ferraris win!

Edwin Wilson (8)
Austin Friars St Monica's School

My Little Doggy Sparky

Sparky is a doggy whose hair is very rough
But every time she barks at me
She doesn't sound too tough!
'Why,' you ask, 'is this the case?'
If she is very rough
The answer is quite simple that
When she barks, she goes . . .
Yip, yap, yap, yip, yap, yip!
Instead of *woof, woof!*

Maya Alberti (8)
Austin Friars St Monica's School

The King Cobra's Attack - Haiku

The king cobra waits
For its poisonous attack
Strike! The mouse is dead!

John Colwell (8)
Austin Friars St Monica's School

The Dragon - Haiku

Here comes the dragon
Just look at all those sharp teeth
And the burning fire.

Ailsa Duncan (7)
Austin Friars St Monica's School

Leaves - Haiku

Leaves are falling down
They slowly dance, round and round
Their colours are brown.

William Ferdinand (7)
Austin Friars St Monica's School

The Planet - Haiku

The planet spins round
The planet spins very fast
Round and round it goes.

Isabella Harrison (7)
Austin Friars St Monica's School

Volcano - Haiku

Volcano burns bright
Spitting fire into the night
I warn you, *beware!*

Thomas Harrison (8)
Austin Friars St Monica's School

The Rabbit - Haiku

The fast rabbit runs
The rabbit is very small
Rabbit likes to hop.

Jane Irving (7)
Austin Friars St Monica's School

Horses - Haiku

Wonderful horses
They gallop and jump today
Quickly now, watch them.

Isabel Leitch (7)
Austin Friars St Monica's School

Tornadoes - Haiku

Whirling round and round,
Through the windy blackened sky
Whirl! Back it has gone.

Joseph Logue (8)
Austin Friars St Monica's School

The Attack Of The Blue Shark - Haiku

The sly great blue shark
The terror it brings to fish
Snap! In goes the fish.

Bruce Long (8)
Austin Friars St Monica's School

The Great White Shark - Haiku

The sly great white shark
Is gliding in the water
Its teeth kill a fish.

Daniel Lumb (8)
Austin Friars St Monica's School

The Grizzly Bear - Haiku

The grizzly bear waits
It plunges in the water.
Swipe! The fish is dead!

Rory Sutton (8)
Austin Friars St Monica's School

-

The Volcano - Haiku

The volcano bursts.
Lava smashes under rocks.
An explosion bangs!

Christian Wood (7)
Austin Friars St Monica's School

The Wolf - Haiku

Running through the trees
The wolf is very hungry.
Bite! The boar is dead.

Adrian Anderson (7)
Austin Friars St Monica's School

Volcano - Haiku

Volcanoes erupt.
Lava can flow very fast.
It can melt metal.

Harry Blowing (8)
Austin Friars St Monica's School

Greedy Monkey - Haiku

Swinging through the trees
Searching for something to eat,
Found a big mango.

Georgina Clough (7)
Austin Friars St Monica's School

Thunder Rumble - Haiku

Rumbling and grumbling
Nobody gets out if the
Thunder is about.

Oskar Nicholson (8)
Austin Friars St Monica's School

The Elephant - Haiku

Rolling in the swamp
Getting all wet and muddy
Shoots water from trunk.

Kathryn Orr (8)
Austin Friars St Monica's School

Slipping Penguin- Haiku

Slipping on the ice.
Swimming fast to catch some fish
Munching fish for tea.

Molly Pattinson (7)
Austin Friars St Monica's School

The Leopard - Haiku

The hungry leopard
Chasing the quick antelope
Pounce and eat it quick.

May Percival (7)
Austin Friars St Monica's School

The Eagle - Haiku

Flying in the air
Spots a small mouse down below
Swoops down, dinner time!

Rupert Rosindell (8)
Austin Friars St Monica's School

The Sly Snake - Haiku

He was slithering
Camouflaging in the grass
Preparing to kill.

Ellie Routledge (7)
Austin Friars St Monica's School

The Hungry Wolf - Haiku

He's ready to pounce
At any time of the day
The wolf cries out loud.

Martin Wright (8)
Austin Friars St Monica's School

Jealousy

Jealousy, other people's praise
It's just like being trapped in a green maze
Jealousy, you want it to stop
It keeps on coming and suddenly *pop!*
Jealousy, you lose friends over it
It's just like having a bright green fit
Jealousy, it's not that nice
It's just like being on bright green ice!

Gemma Stacey (10)
Austin Friars St Monica's School

Dancing

I like dancing
Springy bouncing.
I like dancing
Always prancing.
Toe tap, hop step
I like dancing.

Melissa Chesterman (9)
Gosforth CE Primary School

Number Poem

One obese ostrich sitting in the sun,
Two tantrumming tortoise having no fun.
Three thumping thumpers thumping on the beach,
Four fiddling ferrets with twenty sweets each.
Five fat falcons falling from the sky,
Six sad seagulls swimming with a fly.
Seven sick saints playing football,
Eight angry elephants going to the mall.
Nine hasty monkeys climbing some trees,
Ten tickling tigers flicking off fleas.

Adam Aldridge (10)
Gosforth CE Primary School

The Pencil

Pencils are big,
Pencils are small,
Pencils can be incredibly tall.

Pencils are thick,
Pencils are thin,
You need a big pot to keep them in.

Rub, rub, rub,
And pop it in your big tub.

William Hughes (10)
Gosforth CE Primary School

There Was A Young Boy From France

There was a young boy from France
Who thought he might take a chance.
He went to the sea,
Got stung by a bee,
And then did a fine Irish dance.

Joe Barker (9)
Gosforth CE Primary School

The Sea

From the clouds it took white fluff
And from the storm lightning.
Then the tree gave it green
And ink gave it blue.
The crash of the waves tipped with foam
All but drove the tsunami home.
It toyed with the houses, the churches and steeples,
Leaving a trail of destruction and hurting the people.
It crashed and it boomed like a towering wall,
Leaving the people feeling so small!

And a new sound was heard amongst the terrible din
Above the wailing of voices and moaning for kin.
A long buzz from the darkening sky
As a three-bladed monster built just to fly
Landed on the ground
Emergency help spilling out and around.

Joseph Smith (9)
Gosforth CE Primary School

The Meaning Of Life

The meaning of life
Is not leaving your wife,
But at the blade of a knife
When you cut the bread
You stand in a shed.
You see a cloud, only you should view.
Nothing to scream at, nothing to boo.
Unless you see it in the loo
Not a single clue.

Scott Vandepeear (10)
Gosforth CE Primary School

Late Again Possy

(Inspired by 'Excuses, Excuses' by Gareth Owen)

'Late again, Possy?
What's the excuse this time?'
'My mum went on holiday, Sir'
'But what about your dad?'
'He's asleep, Sir.'
'Why is he asleep?'
'He works nights, Sir.'
'Where's the alarm clock?'
'We don't have one, Sir.'
'Why don't you have one?'
'I never thought about one, Sir.'
'Do you have any sisters Possy?'
'Yes, seven, Sir.'
'Why didn't they wake you up?'
'Because we don't have an alarm clock!'

Lauren Dawson (10)
Gosforth CE Primary School

Sound

The cry of a baby
The growl of a bear
The turn in the lock
And the scrape of a chair.

The bang of a door,
The wind on the pane,
The whistle of the kettle,
The dripping of a drain.

The buzz of the boiler,
The ring of the phones,
The creak of a shelf
And my brother always moans.

Dani Lewis (9)
Gosforth CE Primary School

Jonny Wilkinson

Great player,
Ball passer,
Goal kicker,
Hard trainer,
Conversion getter,
Big hitter,
World Cup winner,
Try scorer,
Trophy holder,
Team player,
My idol,
England fly-half,
The most competitive man in the world.

Sam Farrar (10)
Gosforth CE Primary School

Me And My Dog

My dog loves me.
If I keep sitting here I could get some food.
He's really athletic.
I lay around in the sun sniffing the grass.
I put him on his lead.
This lead is too tight.
He trots proudly to the park.
Do we have to go in here?
He loves children.
That girl has a biscuit in her pocket.
We go home and he rests quietly.
I chew the furniture.
We both go to sleep.
I jump on his bed.
My dog loves me.

Kathleen Coverley Naylor (10)
Gosforth CE Primary School

Conversation Poem

(Inspired by 'Excuses, Excuses' by Gareth Owen)

'Late again, Clarke?
What's the excuse this time?'
'Not my fault, Sir.'
'Whose fault is it then?'
'My cat's, Sir.'
'What did it do?'
'It got squashed, Sir.'
'Squashed, where at?'
'On the road, Sir.
She's dead, alright!'
'That makes four excuses this term and all on gymnastic days.'
'I know, it's very upsetting, Sir.'
'How do you explain it then?'
'The postman came and knocked on the door and said your cat's
                                                    been squashed,

That's what happened, Sir.'
'Where is it now?'
'In the fridge, Sir.'
'What's it doing in there?'
'It keeps it fresh, Sir.'
'This is the last time I want you to be late, Clarke, now scram!'

Georgia Clarke (9)
Gosforth CE Primary School

My Baby Brother

My baby brother, as loud as can be,
My baby brother, just like me.
My baby brother crawls around the house,
My baby brother ratches like a mouse.
My baby brother is tractor daft,
My baby brother likes to be bathed.
My baby brother likes to wiggle,
My baby brother likes to giggle.
My baby brother likes to honk the horn,
My baby brother is . . . Matthew John Osborn!

Grant Mounsey (11)
Gosforth CE Primary School

There Was A Small Girl From Big Rig

There was a small girl from Big Rig,
Who had a rather large pet pig.
It drank ten litres
And ran four metres,
And that was the freakish pet pig!

Kate Mitchell (9)
Gosforth CE Primary School

The Song

Songs of thoughts, songs of heart,
Songs that have a word at the start.
We won't be long, just a jiffy,
Some are sad, some are funny.
Some are short, some are long,
Now that's what I call a song!
Some songs are sung by pop stars,
Some music comes from horns off a car.
Most people come from the cities
To hear the loud fantasy!
Let's sing our song out today,
Let's dance to it all day!

Callum Atkinson (10)
Gosforth CE Primary School

Farm

F is for fords and fences
A is for animals, calves, pigs and sheep
R is for Ronald's big orange machines
M is for machines, mechanical and movable.

Andrew Hilton (11)
Gosforth CE Primary School

Dog Or Cat

From a cute friendly dog
To a ferocious wild cat.
From a nice warm cosy kennel with a toy rubber bone
To deep down in the jungle on a tree branch alone.
From walkies and running every single day
To bouncing and pouncing on prey.
From huggles, snuggles and sloppy licks
To dark piercing eyes and sharp blade-like teeth.

Erin Marley (11)
Gosforth CE Primary School

Fred Is Late Again

'Late again, Fred?'
'Yes, Sir.'
'What this time?'
'Mum, Sir.'
'What about Mum?'
'Late, Sir.'
'For what, Fred?'
'For work, Sir.'
'Then what about Friday? Art?'
'Bully, Sir.'
'What did he do?'
'Locked me in the locker, Sir.'
'What is his name?'
'Not allowed to say, Sir.'
'Why not?'
'He'll kill me, Sir.'
'OK then, what about yesterday, Fred?'
'Nothing, Sir.'
'Nothing?'
'No Sir, I made everything up, Sir.'

Allard Newell (10)
Gosforth CE Primary School

Misunderstanding

The fire roared a ferocious roar,
Lashing its flames at the cliff tops.
The teacher wrote a little note
'You forgot all your full stops'
The little boy shivered in the dark and gloomy wood
Where the dead men hung.
The teacher wrote a little note
She thought they were shot by a gun.
The cannons acted, the muskets fired
At the battle of Medokiate.
The teacher wrote a little note,
'Exclamation marks would be appropriate'
The siren, loud, the planes roared,
As the bombers flew ahead.
The teacher wrote a little note,
'Most German soldiers are dead'
Now hang on a minute
I write a good story and the teacher marks it wrong?
It's just a little mistake,
Teachers, I'll never understand them.

Pepijn van den Elzen (9)
Gosforth CE Primary School

Autumn

Autumn snuck out and made people put on their coats again
Dropping leaves off trees.
Autumn danced through the whispering winds,
Turning flowers and leaves a beautiful golden brown.
Autumn fought his way through summer
Turning winds crisp and leaves golden-brown
And then he *died!*

Bethany Murray (10)
Greengate Junior School

Autumn

Autumn crept through the woods
Like a smooth tiger dashing through the leaves on a dark street
                                                    of silence.
Autumn danced around and around
Like the leaves and now the sun has gone and the wind is out.
Autumn whispered through the trees,
Nice and quietly to know that there's no one there and winter
                                                    is his death.

Debeny McPoland (10)
Greengate Junior School

The Killer Fork

A cereal killer
Satan's trident
The one and only Bart Simpson
A vicious tiger waiting to kill its prey
Stab anything in its tracks
An unstoppable killer.

Danielle Hardman (11)
Greengate Junior School

The Fork

A spear that stabs through hunger.
A hand that reaches out and strikes its target.
The boy that is Bart Simpson.
The sharp teeth of a crocodile.
The sword in the mash.
The eagle devouring its prey.
A deadly mob clearing the plate.

Jay Cresswell (10)
Greengate Junior School

Limerick

There once was an old man from Spain,
Who thought he had a very big brain.
So he went to the shops,
To buy some pork chips,
Then posted them down the drain.

Sam Loughran (10)
Greengate Junior School

A Fork

A metal panther's claws ready to strike!
The bars of a gloomy prison.
A sword shining in the sun.
A roller coaster zooming fast!
An old man's hand.

Sam Pickering (11)
Greengate Junior School

Fork

A hedgehog collecting your food.
A shining sword in the hot sun.
A spade digging for food.
A dragon claw scratching his enemies.

David Morgan (10)
Greengate Junior School

Gas Kills - Cinquain

Gas kills
Save animals
Stop global warming *now!*
Recycle, reuse, reduce more!
Climate!

Chloe Smith (10)
Greengate Junior School

A Woman From Barrow

There was a young lady of Barrow,
Who owned a group of sparrows.
She overfed them,
They found her gold gem
And flew far away from Barrow!

Lauren Purcell (11)
Greengate Junior School

The Climate - Cinquain

Reduce!
Reuse those shoes.
The climate needs your help.
The world would be much happier,
Change it!

Jason Caine (11)
Greengate Junior School

Help! - Cinquains

Gasses
Destroying land
Ice land melting away
Creatures and humans affected
Wasting.

Transport
Puffing out fumes
Factories with big gas
Add to the crumbling atmosphere
Deadly.

Ryan Sharkey (11)
Greengate Junior School

The Fork

A steel dragon attacking its prey.
A silver assassin waiting in the shadowy draw.
A metallic catapult shooting food in your mouth.
A four-pronged sword preparing to kill.
A titan of terror for food everywhere
A four-armed alien zapping your lunch.

Connor Reid (10)
Greengate Junior School

Crazy Man

There once was an old man from Norway
Who always stood in the toilet doorway.
When people tried to get through
He said, 'Do you need the loo?'
That crazy old man from Norway.

Steven Logan (11)
Greengate Junior School

Awakening Gargoyles

Creaking floorboards
Moving gargoyles
One foot moves
You carry on walking
You look
He's not there
You turn around
He gives you a scare!

Liam Pollard (10)
Greengate Junior School

Trapped

There I was abandoned in a deep dark dungeon.
Strange noises echoed around the musty room.
All I could see was a fire fox crying for help,
A flute master going backwards in time to save his groups.
I heard an evil voice saying, 'The food of the moon is mine!'

Morgan Bowes (10)
Greengate Junior School

Dungeon

All is gloomy, dark and damp.
We only have one flute, three snakes and five balls.
The red one will keep us safe
But will it help us with our quest
Where two snakes defeat the fox?
The Snake Lord kills for he eats meat.
At twelve tonight his snakes are free
To roam these dark and gloomy dungeons.

Jordan Kenrick (10)
Greengate Junior School

Doomed

We were trapped in the wind of time
Backwards and forwards.
Eat the food of the moon.
Watch the spiders,
Watch the snakes.
Snake Lord is strong
When moonlight strikes
So beware of everything and anything!

Rebekka Heslop (10)
Greengate Junior School

The Future Is Mine!

The flute's sound was as sharp as wind touching your bare skin,
The future was as if you were falling, falling deeper into a dream.
With a crash, I touched the ground.
The future was in my palms.
Gazing wonderfully at my kingdom, I realised there's no place
like home.

Hayley Williams (10)
Greengate Junior School

The Old Days

A deep, dark dungeon
A fearsome snake lord
The flute master
The food of the moon
The brave fire fox
The hidden key.

Abby Readhead (10)
Greengate Junior School

The Hunt

Skeletons on the wall,
A man in armour who does not walk or talk.
The dark, damp dungeon for them all
And we feast till dawn.

Abigail Hardie (10)
Greengate Junior School

Prisoner In My Own Castle

I am a prisoner in my own castle.
No one but me in the dungeon,
I am a prisoner in my own castle.
Somehow I must break free!
I am a prisoner in my own castle.
Rats scurrying, hunting for food.
I am a prisoner in my own castle.

Jemma Young (11)
Greengate Junior School

Back In Time, A Medieval Experience

As I stole through the dungeon
With hungry wolves howling,
The bats flew around the room.
Black widow spider climbed up the walls.
Snakes slithered on the floor.
As the wolves came closer,
I smelt the human flesh around their mouths.

Chantelle Mayor (11)
Greengate Junior School

The Dungeon

The dungeon black and unwanted,
Water from the roof slipping down our faces.
We looked around but can't reveal the answer to our quest.
Spiders spinning a web from every possible corner.
Fire Fox looked up too, we're both going to die
In the dungeon, black and unwanted.

Jodie Leonard (11)
Greengate Junior School

Back To The Future

In a dungeon lived a prince
And his pet, the fire fox
Trapped like a rat.
We must get out!
Spiders creeping up the walls
Oozing slime dripping down the cage.
I can hardly move knowing the snake lord is watching.

Jesse Powell (10)
Greengate Junior School

The Dungeon

We're trapped in the dungeon.
It is so cold, so damp.
Spiders crawling through the cracks in the wall.
The chains on my arms are rusty,
Only have till midnight.
However will we get out?

Nathan Jasper (11)
Greengate Junior School

Medieval Experience

Rattling chains
Damp and smelly
We're trapped, nowhere to go
Nothing to do.

Snakes and spiders galore
Fearless prince
Two key pieces
Flute Master takes it away.

Victory at last
A glorious feast
Scrumptious chicken
And lovely mead.

Nikki Weall (10)
Greengate Junior School

Summer - Cinquains

The heat
Shines upon us
But unnecessary
Summer shower doused our feelings.
Come back.

Quickly
The time goes by,
As the sunshine fades slow
The showers are looming up high.
Downpour.

Vanessa Graham (10)
Greengate Junior School

Teacher

Think they're clever
Whatever!
Some tall
Some small
Deep thinker
Coffee drinker
SATS they adore
Work galore
Spell checker
Always better
Checks books
Gives funny looks
Has a great smile
If a child takes a while
Children sharer
Knowledge sharer.

Cathy Rawlings (10)
Greengate Junior School

My Dog - Cinquains

My dog
Is brown and white
And fluffy all over
Playful and active, never stops.
But then . . .

She sleeps
By the fire
Until the next morning
There she will stay cosy and warm
Peaceful.

Lauren Edwards (11)
Greengate Junior School

Sportsman Kennings

Basketball striker
Football defender
Champion swimmer
Fast runner
Older brother
Temper loser
Sweet eater
Music lover
Dog teaser
Cat lover
Neat colourer
Trampoline bouncer.

Sam Crawford (11)
Greengate Junior School

Seasons

Summer
Lazy mornings
Splashing in the water
Having fun with my best friends
Cooling

Winter
Freezing mornings
By the crackling fire
Wrap up in warm fleecy jacket
Cosy.

Kimberley Sayle (11)
Greengate Junior School

What Am I? - Kennings

Face licker
Bone chewer
Belly tickler
Teddy ripper
Tail wagger
Bath escaper
Meat eater
Water drinker
Cat chaser
Fast runner
Clue: *woof, woof!*

Chloe Hilton (10)
Greengate Junior School

That's Me Kennings

Fast runner
Art maker
Swimming lover
Work taker
Trampoline jumper
Rugby hater
Maths liker
Basketball striker
Friend maker
Smile blusher
Book reader
Sandwich eater.

Michaela Halliday (11)
Greengate Junior School

Doctor Who - Doomsday - Cinquains

Daleks
The Cybermen
Killed people for the Earth,
Extracted brainwaves, now trapped in
The Void.

Delete!
Exterminate!
The killer chants were called.
Dalek Sec temporal shifted
Away.

Matthew Lightfoot (10)
Greengate Junior School

Nia's Kennings

Netball lover
Goal shooter
Athletics runner
Animal liker
Glasses hater
Soap watcher
Football hater
Book reader
That's me!

Nia Studt (10)
Greengate Junior School

Big Cat Kennings

Sharp biter
Meat tearer
Tail swisher
Fast runner
Fur comber
Wash lover
Tongue flicker
High jumper
Sun soaker
Loud roarer
Claw scratcher
Fierce fighter.

Brandon Edmondson (10)
Greengate Junior School

Guess Who?

Bully hater
Ice skater
Scotland lover
Cool brother
Drama queen
Sometimes mean
Liverpool supporter
Drinking water
Great shopper
Bad hopper
Present ringer
Good singer
Little prancer
Brilliant dancer.

Irene Courtney (11)
Greengate Junior School

All About Me

Pet lover
Numeracy know all
Bolton supporter
Friend maker
Science hater
Swimming fan
School lover
Play admirer
Brother hater
Liverpool liker
Bike rider
Chocolate lover.

Ashleigh Lancaster (10)
Greengate Junior School

That's Me - Cinquain

Watters
Good footy boy
A brilliant runner
Favourite food, chicken curry
That's me!

Nathan Watters (11)
Greengate Junior School

Seasonal - Haikus

Winter
We wear scarves and gloves
Everything is cold as ice
We stay by the fire.

Spring
All plants come to life
Everywhere the flowers bloom
The Earth comes to life.

Lauren Doherty (10)
Greengate Junior School

Calcium

Pizza lover
Poker player
Simpsons watcher
Chelsea supporter
Footy crazy
Snooker lover
Maltesers cruncher
Bag puncher.

Callum Lloyd (10)
Greengate Junior School

Seasonal - Haikus

Summer
The heat is violent
There are no clouds in my sight
It is piping hot.

Autumn
Leaves float down from trees
Colours red, yellow and brown
Run through the forest.

James Dodgson (11)
Greengate Junior School

Darco The ?

Flame thrower
Huge grower
Fire maker
Ground shaker
Hell bringer
Smell linger
Poison inserts
Fireball diverts
Claws clash
Teeth smash.

Dean Fennemore Wilson (11)
Greengate Junior School

Creature - Haikus

Dragons
Bloodthirsty creatures
Venomous fangs destroy all
They kill by instinct.

Spiders
Creepy-crawly legs
Creeping round your property
Legs long and hairy.

Lions
Vicious pounding paws
Destroys anything alive
Mane is long and thick.

Jordan Twinney (11)
Greengate Junior School

The Warm And The Cold

Rising sun melts the frozen morning
And the crystals of ice glitter like hidden fairies.
Ghostly trees reach above the mist, hanging above the burbling river
Like knotted fingers reaching to the crimson sky.
A rabbit twitches warm and cosy in its burrow
While friends breathe clouds of ice in the frosty crack of dawn.
A worm embedded in the earth like a cherry on a cake,
Deer on a hillside like a furry wind break.
The moon reaches forward and disappears down a hill
And the sun leaps to the air, lighting the bleak sky.
Vines twist and writhe in the morning breeze
Wind chimes clang and clatter in the swirling torrents of air

Sunlight flashes on windows and bounces off the goat's bright eyes.
Cries echo from the calling deer as they catch sight of the
colossal light.
A rainbow flickers through the clouds
For the rain is softly cascading, running from the sun.
The fox darts into the sunrise, a spirit fleeing from the night.
Owls settle to sleep as most creatures stumble into a new day.
The crowd knocks a slate off the roof as it wakes clumsily
The new day blinding him, sending him into a new nightmare.
The sky fades from red to blue, a glittering blue like a canvas of
sapphires.
A gannet swoops low and clashes into the river sending a thin layer
of ice flying through the air.
A hedgehog emerges from the mouldy leaves damp and musty
As the morning emerges bright as a toddler's eyes.

Eve Turner (11)
Hunter Hall School

Silent Is The Dewy Dawn

Silent is the dewy dawn,
The reaching trees like silver,
Moon nor sun lies in the heavens,
Everything is empty,
No one is there or so it seems.

A tiny slender face gazes from the soft grass.
A flawless face, a clever face with lively knowing eyes of gold,
The fairy, with hair of reddish-brown, dances out into the open earth,
Then another, another!
Delicate creatures dancing and singing in bewitching,
                              spellbinding voices,
In garments of brilliant colours, embroidered with flowers and tiny
                                    silver pebbles,
With flimsy butterfly wings, folded behind their backs.
They have been to so many places and seen so much and known
                              so much!
The slender creatures dart to the sky,
Gleaming like fireflies, curving and spiralling away into the orange sky.

Silent is the dewy dawn,
The reaching trees like silver,
Moon nor sun lies in the heavens,
Everything is empty,
No one is there or so it seems.

Kiera Davidson (11)
Hunter Hall School

The Magic Box

(Based on 'Magic Box' by Kit Wright)

I shall put in my box . . .
The autumn leaves falling off bare trees
The red of the ripe tomatoes,
The crisp bite of a red rosy apple.

I shall put in the box . . .
The damp smell on a misty morning,
The farmer in the golden fields cutting corn,
The rainfall on a damp green leaf.

I shall put in my box . . .
The long working hours of the poor as they pick fruit from trees,
The crisp taste of a ripe pear,
The buzz of a crowded market square.

I shall put in my box . . .
The pitter-patter of the rain on an autumn morning,
The golden corn,
A rainbow arching above the trees and fields.

My box is made from a thousand raindrops
A ray of sun and an arching rainbow.
I shall cure the sick in my box.

Jenny Marsh (11)
Hunter Hall School

The Spirit Of Christmas

Christmas tree lights gleaming out of frosty windows,
People zooming down snowy hills in their sledges,
Home-made mince pies fresh from the oven
Families queuing up to get their Christmas dinner meat
And me piercing open that first tasty chocolate from my
                                         Advent calendar.

Choirs knocking on doors singing Christmas carols so tunefully
The loud church bells ringing through my ears as Christmas is coming
Parties with loud music and laughter and champagne bottles
                                         popping open
Rustling wrapping paper being used for presents
And crackers banging open as paper hats fly everywhere.

The warming scent of Christmas puddings
The promise of brandy butter dribbling
Burning coal as it sits in the fire smouldering to smithereens
The yummy warmed-up mince pies have just been bitten in to
The roast goose crackling in the oven with lots of seasoning and
The Christmas tree pines have an aromatic smell which fills up
                                         the house.

My thoughts are of decorations from the attic
It's freezing outside, will it snow?
Are the reindeer ready for their long journey?
I can't believe it, is Christmas really here?
Remembering such a special boy being born a long time ago.

Ella Tennant (11)
Hunter Hall School

The Traveller's Fate!

Snarling, howling lay a dog,
Through the swirling mist and fog.

No longer could the traveller see,
What would happen? What would be?

No one could tell or foresee,
What this dog would turn out to be.

Closer still the traveller got
His horse breaking into a steady trot.

Its eyes were blazing,
Its teeth so white, so amazing.

Slowly sweat was dripping down,
Mist swirling like a crown.

It sprung up, tail lashing,
Big jaws gnashing, slowly crashing.

In the night so dark and hard,
The man rode away deeply scarred.

He went swiftly into the night,
Soon he had rode out of sight.

The night again was dark and still,
A bird sat on a window sill.

Not a soul knew what had happened
Apart from the hedgerows and the bracken.

Arabella Sharrock (10)
Hunter Hall School

Moving On

The sea is calm and oh so blue
All around me everything is new.
It's all so quiet
There is no noise,
Me and my sisters
Can play safe with our toys.

The rooms keep on going
The gardens are vast,
Such a huge change
From our home in the past.

No noisy neighbours,
No barking dogs,
No blue lights flashing
From the police driving past.

The wind, our hair blowing
Our kites flying high,
The clouds are all fluffy
As they dance by.

I smile and I'm happy,
I'm as free as a bird,
My life is beginning
To take a new curve.

When I am older,
I can look back and say
All our lives changed
When we moved away.

Katrina Weightman (10)
Hunter Hall School

The Golden Giraffe Trophy

The clock struck 10.40, the bell followed with an energetic sound,
harsh upon the ear!
Brutal rhinos hurtled through the dim red door, making an obvious
cavity into the solid stone,
Which was the entrance to the most dreadful of nightmares . . .
the playground!

The air was humid; you could smell the tension wafting through
their widened nostrils,
They were off!
The buffalos, the cheetahs, the elephants and the tigers were panting
within strides of each other,
The Golden Giraffe Trophy was sparkling from the dazzling hot sun,
First, second, third, fourth places were awarded as follows,
The tigers, the buffalos and the elephants
But the cheetahs had to live up to their name.
They cheated, but I can't reveal how, it was messy.
I can't say any more, my lips are sealed.
The award goes to . . . 'The Tigers!' roared the lion, holding the trophy
out for grabs.

Then, that moment the bell rang,
They all groaned, like when you have to get up from your restless night
Reluctantly, they returned to their normal lesson only to be met
by their head teacher!

Naomi Sutton (11)
Hunter Hall School

My Harvest Box

(Based on 'Magic Box' by Kit Wright)

I will put in the box . . .
The biggest combine harvester,
The gorgeous fruit pies
And dusty barns to sweep.

I will put in the box . . .
Bright colourful flowers,
Planting vegetables
And the blowing fields of wheat.

I will put in the box . . .
Glittering green grass,
Dirty busy farmers
And the growing fruit trees.

I will put in the box . . .
Tractors collecting crops,
The noisy animals to feed
And the plants to water.

My box is fashioned from dry bails
With early mornings on the lid, shining sun in the corners,
Covered with leaves for my latch.
I shall surf off Africa along the sea
Then get washed in a wheat field and thirst for water and me.

Yasmine Hughes (11)
Hunter Hall School

Harvest Box

(Based on 'Magic Box' by Kit Wright)

I will put in the box . . .
The laughter of happy children,
The river playing down a hill,
Grateful people who have waited for this time
And a farmer that loves his people very much.

I will put in the box . . .
Teeth crunching berries and oats,
Spades digging in the soft soil
And a wish from poor people who have nothing but themselves.

I will put in the box . . .
Dancing rain that lets the fruit grow naturally,
Harvest mice that run in the fields as fast as lightning and as slow
                                        as sound
And a beautiful red sunrise.

I will put in the box . . .
Trees with leaves all different colours,
Seasons with flowers, glowing suns and misty lakes,
Windy mornings and stormy days
And rainbows of all colours that glitter in the sunlight.

My box is made out of hay, metal and flowers
With laughter on the lid and wishes in the corners.
Its hinges are the unbreakable bond of an acorn and an oak tree
And inside is a harvest festival that will never end.

I will travel in my box to the poorer countries
And bring my harvest with me so there can be happiness once again.

Caitlin McMillan (10)
Hunter Hall School

What Am I?

I wail in the vicious nights
Destructing everything in my sight.
When you see rain I am calling,
I distract the sleeping with my bawling.
You cannot see me but see what I've caused,
Don't you wish that I'd ever pause
And never come back, the end of me,
I have to come sometimes, don't you see!
I am the partner of the rain and cold,
When they come you see my effects bold.
Keep out of my way and I can't hurt you,
But if you come near I'll blow you through!

What am I?
A windstorm.

Francesca Wilcox (10)
Hunter Hall School

Summer

Summer brings light, warmth and happiness.
It brings luscious crops, green trees and lush meadows.
It brings time to rest, long light days.
But there is a dark side to it.
It brings drought and starvation.
But it tries to make people happy when it can.

Rui Bashall (11)
Hunter Hall School

My Harvest Poem

(Based on 'Magic Box' by Kit Wright)

I will put in my box . . .
The wind blowing the long golden crops,
The sun making the beautiful tulips grow,
The clouds spitting down the cold water from the sky.

I will put in my box . . .
The rivers flowing down the misted hills,
Fishes that have been caught up in the crusted nets,
People picking the rosy-red apples.

I will put in my box . . .
Children too weak to feed themselves,
The look on the farmer's face seeing his crops fail,
All of the vegetables not growing to be big enough.

I will put in my box . . .
The smell of all the ripe fruit,
The first look from a newborn calf,
The lambs taking their first steps.

My box is magnificent gold shaped into a star
With mystical things in the corners.
The lid is safely put on to keep the magical things inside.

I shall fly in my box over the oceans to Africa to give it to
                                    the poor people
I turn their glum faces to happy faces.

Charlotte Ward (10)
Hunter Hall School

My Special Box

(Based on 'Magic Box' by Kit Wright)

I will put in my box . . .
The strength of a thrush pulling a worm,
Loud birdsong in the early morning,
The flowers swaying in the light wind
Water keeping all living things alive.

I will put in my box . . .
Pears and apples ripening in the boiling sun,
Fruit and vegetables eaten slowly and happily,
All that's shared at markets and stores,
The golden corn sways in the wind like dancers.

I will put in my box . . .
The thud of a tangerine falling from a woven basket,
Bubbling damson jam in a shiny pot,
A field mouse carrying a plump blackberry to his family,
Grasshoppers jump-racing through the cut wheat.

I will put in my box . . .
The warm rays of the late summer sun,
A red robin hopping about fattening up for winter,
The sweet aroma of grapes turning into wine,
The smell of freshly baked bread slipping into my nose.

My box is made from woven grass,
Corn heads peep out of the corners,
Pressed leaves and flowers make the lid,
A story lies hidden in every nook and cranny.

I shall make peace in my box wherever I go
Travelling around the universe and give seeds to those in need.

Max Laszlo (10)
Hunter Hall School

My Special Box

(Based on 'Magic Box' by Kit Wright)

I will put in my box . . .
The wheat in the fields swaying in the wind,
And the corn standing proud and tall in the moonlight.
I will put the sun in my box burning bright as it makes things grow.
I will capture the raindrops as they fall from the sky and put them
in my box.
I will put all the fruits of the world mixed together into one small
tasty fruit in my box.
I will put all the vegetables from around the globe mixed into one
special tasty vegetable.
I will keep famine locked away in my box to stop people starving
in the world.
All the starving people in the world can come and live in my box
and eat all my healthy food.
I will make my box out of the stars, clutched from the galaxy.
When I step into my box, I will be flying in the universe visiting
all the planets.

Harry Towers (10)
Hunter Hall School

My Magic Box

(Based on 'Magic Box' by Kit Wright)

I will put in my box . . .
The first cry of a swallow sweeping through the barns,
The first sight of a poppy in the meadows,
The first sound of lambs bleating in the fields,
The first sheaves of wheat bobbing in the distance.

I will put in my box . . .
The smell of freshly mown grass, ready for winter feed,
Summer storms flattening the wheat and corn,
Blackberries, sloes and blueberries growing freshly in the hedgerows,
Flowers showing everywhere you look.

I will put in my box . . .
The blinding light of the sun,
The madness of farmers with faulty machinery,
The sound of the combine harvester working the way through the corn,
Bright green leaves growing on the trees.

I will put in my box . . .
The sight of wheat piled high in the sheds,
The smell of the fruit pies cooking in the Aga,
Children playing in the brown rustling leaves,
The waterlogged field stopping the farmers from ploughing.

My magic box is fashioned from wood of an old oak tree,
Jewels made from acorns and sheaves of wheat cover the lid.

I shall fly in my box over brown ploughed fields
Then land on a branch and watch squirrels collect their winter feed.

Hannah Addison (10)
Hunter Hall School

The Harvest Box

(Based on 'Magic Box' by Kit Wright)

I will put in my box . . .
The diseases of the world,
The excitement in a happy man's heart,
A thud from an apple falling.

I will put in my box . . .
Gold cornfields,
The winter rain,
The harvest choir.

I will put in my box . . .
The scent from a pineapple,
The smoke from a factory,
A table full of vegetables.

I will put in my box . . .
The black night of autumn,
The sun's rays,
A butterfly.

Daniel Richardson (10)
Hunter Hall School

Out To Play

The silence is coming,
Into the playground, up the swings,
Down the slide, spreading calmly,
Far and wide.

Then suddenly,
The swings go creak
And heard above the noise,
Is the tiny patter of children's feet.

Then into the playground they do rush to scream
And run and make a fuss,
The bedraggled teacher does but say,
'No going on the grass, today!'

But hey,
Do the children take heed?
No I say, no siree.

On the grass they run
And up the trees to have some fun,
Round and round and round
Until the teacher stands her ground
And shouts as loud as she can,
'End of break,
Out, out, out!
Come on children, do not pout!'

Then all falls quiet,
The silence is coming
Into the playground, up the swings,
Down the slide, spreading calmly,
Far and wide.

Theo Simmons (10)
Hunter Hall School

My Pony Pancake

On Saturday my best friend Annie
Came and helped me muck out Pannie.
On went his head collar
But as we tried to tie his rope
Pannie came to follow
His eyes gleaming with hope.
He thought it was time for a trot
But we hadn't tacked him up
So we stood him in the yard
Until we'd moved all of his muck!
Whatever you do, don't disturb him
When he's eating chaff and hay
Or he'll playfully nip and bite you
To send you on your way.

Sarah Waugh (9)
Hunter Hall School

Cross-Country Running

Start line
Gun blow
In a second
Off we go!
First thing
Up a hill
Then we go
Down a hill.
Lungs are panting
Stitch is coming
You can do it
Just keep on running!
Suddenly
I trip and fall
Oh why did I
Start this after all?
I'm almost there
The finish line's in sight
You never know
I just might
But I feel so tired
I've no more breath
My heart is aching
Thank goodness there's no more left!
Somebody's got a
Record time
You will never guess
But it's mine!

Megan Bates (10)
Hunter Hall School

What Is White?

White is a sound
A baby's cry.
White are the clouds
In the blue, blue sky.
White is the feeling
In a silent room,
White is the colour
Of the nice witch's broom.
White is a clean page
Laid down in your book.
White is a bride
With a wonderful look.
White is a show-off,
No doubt about that.
But can you imagine
Living without it?

Katie Leitch (10)
Hunter Hall School

Mountain Biking

In last gear
Up the fell
Tired and hungry
One short breath
Peddling hard
Feel sick
Almost there
Trying hard
Hands are sweaty
Keep on going
A little grip
One short slip
Dog runs past
Very fast
I say
I won't give up
The top is near
Don't look back
The sun is out
On my back
I feel the heat
Not looking back.

Sophie Banks (10)
Hunter Hall School

The Swimming Race

Gun fires
Push off start
Water rushing in your face
Feels like you're pulling a cart
Hardly any space
Pulling hard
Kicking hurts
Red card
Finish line not in sight
Waving, cheering
Clapping, splashing
Can hear
Hair wet
Ears blocked
Stand in sight
Hands, feet and bubbles everywhere
Water in your goggles soaked
Finish line in sight
Must breathe
Chest hurts
Breathing hard, water hearing
Grow weaker
Heartbeat fast
Nearly there
Touch the side, done!

Sarah Addison (9)
Hunter Hall School

What Is Black?

Black are the crows flying high in the sky,
Black is the colour of burnt blueberry pie.
Black is a cat crossing over a wall,
Black is your knee when you have had a fall.
Black is the coal you put on the fire,
Black is a large rubber tyre.
Black is the hole in the universe so high,
Dark is the black, black night sky.

Natalie Fisher (10)
Hunter Hall School

Cumbrian Winter

Hills and fells are frosty and tall
The icy lake looks deep and cold.
In the woods and forests
Squirrels gather all the nuts
Beautiful nature all around.

Icicles hanging from the roofs of cold caves,
Snow drifting high on hills,
Rain flooding all the rivers,
Hail shattering on windows.
The weather is harsh and cruel.

Thick coats, hats and gloves to be worn when walking up the fells,
Cold gales blowing on your face,
Go sledging fast down steep hills all day
Fun things to do in Cumbrian winters.

Sitting in front of a roaring fire
When I'm cold and eating hot pot at teatime
With Mum's home-made biscuits
I love coming home in winter.

Christian Partridge (9)
Hunter Hall School

Cumbrian Winter

Snow-capped fells damp with mist,
Rain crashing on tin roofs.
Forest walks and icy breath,
Crumpets and jam, drop scones and butter.

Lakes are cold with frost and snow,
Gales wail above the dancing trees.
Getting lost in scary caves,
Sitting casually by the fire.

Dark, gloomy forests,
Hail falling like icy swords.
Hiking up the magnificent fells,
My dog is lying on the rug.

The fields are full of huddling sheep,
The snow is falling soft on my cheeks.
Have a ride on the Ullswater steamer,
Feeling cosy in my warm bed.

Elizabeth Relph (9)
Hunter Hall School

Christmas Stocking

Christmas presents
And party lights twinkling
By the fire, pulling
Crackers and finding money
In Christmas puddings.
Soft snow feeling happiness
Inside you, joyful
Toys. When I open
My Christmas presents
My heart fills with joy
And I almost burst.
Smelling Christmas turkey
Laughter fills the house.
Seeing a whole new world
Inside my stocking, marching soldiers
Eating snowy bonbons
Feeling the prick of holly.
The roundness of the orange
Banging on the drum of
Happiness. Decorating the
Christmas tree with holly and
Ivy. Making a white snowman
Waiting for Santa to fill my
Stocking. Grasping the first
Present.

Harry Lowther (9)
Hunter Hall School

Cumbrian Winters

Icy mountains with snow-capped tops
Rigid rocks with glinting ice
Building snowmen
Much more nice!

Wind-smashed boats on stormy lakes
Ropes all tangled underwater
The rescue helicopter braves all weather
Icy mountains, windswept lakes
He will do whatever it takes!

Walking in the crackling snow
We don't mind where we go
Feeding the animals at the gate
Hungry stomachs as they wait!

Boiling kettles on tops of stoves
Wine waiting to be drunk by friends
The cat warms her paws by the fire
Wishing that the flames were higher!

David Absalom (9)
Hunter Hall School

What Is Purple?

I like purple, I don't know why,
I like it so much I could almost cry.
The colour is made with pink and blue,
It's the colour of the rainbow too!
Purple says kind, loving and hugs,
It's also the colour of my pony's rugs.
I love my pony, I now know why,
Purple's the colour when we ride the sky!

Ishbel Lowther (9)
Hunter Hall School

Cumbrian Winter

Snow painted on the tops of hills;
Fresh water running down a slope;
Plants flowing all over the landscape below;
Forests grow like a spot of paint, evergreen.

Gales blow like hundreds of fans blowing at the same time.
Wet tears fall fast and fierce like thunderbolts.
Hail falls like rocks and stones.
Snow falls like a soft blanket, a furry covering of crystals.

Sledging downhill, a fast bullet shooting through the snow;
Making a man of snow as it were clay dough;
Returning home with my family to toast marshmallows by the fire;
Feeling snug and warm on a cosy sofa playing Contraband, Monopoly
and Scrabble,
Smelling the biscuits Mum just made: some for Christmas,
some for now;
Waking up to the first snowflakes of the winter.

Oliver Blackett-Ord (9)
Hunter Hall School

Christmas Stocking

The sparkle of the silver snowflake
Red holly flashing in the distance
Pink, blue, red and yellow toys sitting there
The shiny red of the warm fire
The brown hard wood being burnt away
Black and white fluffy sheep
The snowball of fun and cold
The green trees dancing away
White sparkly doves flying around
Tinsel and glitter glowing
Angels swaying in the breeze.

Olivia Stamper (9)
Hunter Hall School

Cumbrian Winters

Snow-capped fells damp with mist
Rain pattering down
Forest walks and frosted lips
Crumpets and jam in thick socks
Trees shedding golden leaves
Gales threatening to push you over
Steaming across open lakes
Walking high on the mountains
Toasting your toes by the fire
Frozen lakes, icy to touch
Hail coming down like bullets
Caving for hours upon end
As a warm frothy drink of hot chocolate gently lulls you to sleep
The snow goes up over a barren landscape
The snow comes down creating what seems like a world of feathers
Climbing steep rocky cliff faces
Relaxing in a comfortable bed.

Noah Hurton (9)
Hunter Hall School

What Is Pink?

Pink is the colour of flowers.
I hear sounds of pretty tunes that make me think pink.
The feeling of pink lipstick being put on my lips.
Pink is the colour of my pencil case.
Pink is the sound of people talking.
I feel pink roses touch my leg with their velvet petals.
I have a pink T-shirt that I wear at home.
I can hear someone singing which sounds pink.
Pink makes me think!

Millie Holder (9)
Hunter Hall School

I Saw A Jolly Teacher

I saw a jolly teacher
Reading through a book,
She said, 'Come over here,
And have a quick look.'

The book was about a jolly big fountain,
In the jolly blue sky on top of a mountain.

This jolly teacher was my favourite
And was without compare,
But when we went into her lessons,
She was always in despair.

I tried to cheer my teacher up,
But it didn't work at all.
She told me just one jolly thing,
That she had a very bad fall.

Well, that is the end of a jolly day
With my jolly friend called Tess.
Oh, by the way my teacher's name,
Is jolly good old Jess.

Becky Hurst (9)
Hunter Hall School

My Best Friend

Friends are kind
They help you out,
They talk when you are lonely,
They play nice games,
They come to stay,
But . . .
I've one and only friend
She often buys me presents,
She makes me feel so very happy,
When I'm in trouble she's there,
She always holds my hand,
We'll always be together.

Isabella Sharrock (8)
Hunter Hall School

The Sound Collector

(Based on 'The Sound Collector' By Roger McGough)

A person came this afternoon
Dressed all in red and white
He put every sound into a sack
And whisked them out of sight.

The crunching of the picnic,
The banging of the car,
The squeaking of the swing,
The buzzing of the bees.

The howling of the wind,
The rustling of the trees,
The chattering of the children,
The whirring of the car engine.

The crying of the baby,
The singing of the people,
The shouting of the kids,
The barking of the dog.

A person called this afternoon
Stealing every noise he found.
He filled his sack right up to the top
And left us with no sound.

Julia Addison (7)
Hunter Hall School

The Sound Collector

(Based on 'The Sound Collector' By Roger McGough)

A person came this afternoon
Dressed all in red and white
He put every sound into a sack
And whisked them out of sight.

The crying of reception,
The thudding of the shoes,
The laughing of the teachers,
The squeaking of the board pens.

The yelling of the children,
The rustling of the PE bags,
The crunching of the teeth,
The scraping of the fork.

The squishing of the dough,
The swishing of the exam papers,
The screeching of the chairs,
The buzzing of the cars.

A person called this afternoon
Stealing every noise he found.
He filled his sack right to the top
And left us with no sound.

Louisa Evans (7)
Hunter Hall School

The Sound Collector

(Based on 'The Sound Collector' By Roger McGough)

A person came this afternoon
Dressed all in red and white
He put every sound into a sack
And whisked them out of sight.

The creaking of the door,
The shouting of the playground,
The crunching of the courtyard,
The chattering of the children's teeth.

The rustling of the trees,
The banging of the desks,
The singing of the choir,
The screeching of the birds.

The squeaking of the gate,
The revving of the cars,
The whistling of the wind,
The booing of the football.

A person called this afternoon
Stealing every noise he found,
He filled his sack right to the top
And left us with no sound.

Fintan Simmons (7)
Hunter Hall School

The Sound Collector

(Based on 'The Sound Collector' By Roger McGough)

A person came this afternoon
In his pocket there was a little mouse
He put every sound into a sack
And whisked them out of the house.

The creaking of the door,
The singing of the kids,
The shouting of the teacher,
The banging of the desk lids.

The crashing of the table falling over,
The squeaking of the mice,
The scraping of the chairs,
The inkling of the dice.

The screaming of the children,
The whack of the cane,
The crying of the little boy,
The swish of the pony's tail.

A person called this afternoon
Stealing every noise he found.
He filled his sack right to the top
And left us with no sound.

Connie Hurton (7)
Hunter Hall School

The Sound Collector

(Based on 'The Sound Collector' By Roger McGough)

A person came this afternoon
Dressed all in red and white
He put every sound into a sack
And whisked them out of sight.

The chattering of the children,
The banging of the door,
The singing of the choir,
The crashing on the floor.

The whistling of the wind,
The squeaking of the mice,
The shouting of the teacher,
The rolling of the dice.

The rustling of the papers,
The crying of the Reception kids,
The whispering of the trees outside,
The crash of the desk lids.

A person came this afternoon
Stealing every noise he found.
He filled his sack right to the top
And left us with no sound.

Saskia Rockliffe-King (8)
Hunter Hall School

The Sound Collector

(Based on 'The Sound Collector' By Roger McGough)

A person came this afternoon
Dressed all in red and white
He put every sound into a sack
And whisked them out of sight.

The chattering of the teachers,
The shouting of the children,
The squeaking of the mice,
The banging of the desk.

The singing of the choir,
The mumbling of the people,
The creaking of the door,
The rustling of the gravel.

The whistling of the trees,
The cheering of the crowd,
The whirring of the car engine,
The scraping of the chairs.

A person called this afternoon
Stealing every noise he found
He filled his sack right to the top
And left us with no sound.

Sophina Boyd (8)
Hunter Hall School

The Sound Collector

(Based on 'The Sound Collector' By Roger McGough)

A person came this afternoon
Dressed all in red and white
He put every sound into a sack
And whisked them out of sight.

The banging of the doors,
The crying of the baby,
The crunching of the kids eating,
The chattering of the children.

The thudding of the shoes,
The squawking of the cupboards,
The ticking of the clock,
The whispering of the people.

A person came this afternoon
Dressed all in red and white.
He put every sound into a sack
And whisked them out of sight.

Paige-Olivia Lee (7)
Hunter Hall School

Feelings

I saw a bird go flapping by, I felt giddy.
I saw a bird go stamping by, I felt bad.
I saw a bird go fluttering by, I felt happy.
I saw a bird go limping by, I felt sad.
I saw birds soaring high, I felt glad.

James Carruthers (8)   -
Hunter Hall School

The Sound Collector

(Based on 'The Sound Collector' By Roger McGough)

A person came this afternoon
Dressed all in red and white
He put every sound into a sack
And whisked them out of sight.

The chattering of the pupils,
The rusting of the paper,
The whispering of the children,
The squeaking of the ate.

The banging as the gate shuts,
The thudding in the playground,
The munching in the hall,
The singing of the choir.

A person called this afternoon
Stealing every noise he found.
He filled his sack right to the top
And left us with no sound.

Alice Addison (7)
Hunter Hall School

The Sound Collector

(Based on 'The Sound Collector' By Roger McGough)

A person came this afternoon
Dressed all in red and white
He put every sound into a sack
And whisked them out of sight.

The splashing of the wet grass,
The thudding of the ball,
The whistling of the wind,
The squeaking of the trollies.

The rumbling of the clubs,
The banging of the feet,
The cheering for the hole in one,
The chant for a good chip.

A person called this afternoon
Stealing every noise he found.
He filled his sack right to the top
]and left us with no sound.

Nicholas Sowerby (7)
Hunter Hall School

The Water Park

The water park they say
Is very cheap to pay.
Get stuck into heaps of fun
And maybe if lucky, a prize will be won.
The slides go so fast, it's hard to breathe,
When you see that, no way you'll want to leave.
Halfway through why not stop for lunch?
Quick, back to the pool before Mum gives you a nudge.
Hold on tight to the rubber rings,
Sit right up, you'll feel like kings.
The great big dinghy ride, now, that's a whopper,
They're always complaining, it's made out of copper.

Georgia Birley (10)
Hunter Hall School

My Friendly Green Runner Bean

Bouncing on my trampoline
I thought I saw a runner bean.
We bounced and bounced
Just he and me,
I wondered if my mum could see.

Bouncing on my trampoline
My friendly little runner bean
Jumped into the sky,
He flew past clouds and twinkly stars,
He flew right out of sight,
He bumped into an aeroplane
And never said goodnight!

Brook Birley (9)
Hunter Hall School

The Sound Collector

(Based on 'The Sound Collector' by Roger McGough)

A person came this afternoon
Dressed all in red and white,
He put every sound into a sack
And whisked them out of sight.

The singing of the choir,
The rustling of the papers,
The shouting of the children,
The banging of the desks.

The crunching of the adults eating,
The whispering of the wind,
The talking of the people in the playground,
The squeaking of the board pen.

The scraping of the board pen,
The swishing of the trees,
The squawking of the birds,
The whirring of the cars.

A person called this afternoon
Stealing every noise he found,
He filled his sack right to the top
And left us with no sound.

India Birley (7)
Hunter Hall School

The Predator

I can hear the crunching of leaves in the forest as heavy paws pad
the ground.
I can hear them getting closer.
Suddenly it appears from ferns and other tropical plants,
Its deep green eyes staring at me directly.
This creature needs help and so do plenty of others.
Their hearts pounding, the loud eerie noise of machines moving
in their habitat.
The loud bangs of trees crashing to the ground.
Their home is being destroyed.
They are bombarding them, threatening them,
These bloodthirsty, destructive predators are *man!*

Anya Wilcock (10)
Kirkoswald CE Primary School

The Cat

The cat with eyes like diamonds, fur like silk, teeth like knives.
He slips away like a snake.
A cat may be tempting to stroke
But if you're allergic, it's no joke!
When the rash appears it could all end in tears.

Ian Oliver (9)
Kirkoswald CE Primary School

The Loch Ness Monster

Does it exist or is it a myth?
That's what I want to know.
Is it blue, orange or yellow, or perhaps black?
Is it even alive?
I just don't know.
It could be spotty; it could be stripy or even plain.
I just don't know.
I've heard people say again and again,
'I've seen the Loch Ness monster!'
But I still wonder . . .
Does it exist or is it a myth?

Dan Todd (9)
Kirkoswald CE Primary School

The King Of The Jungle

He rises, shakes his golden fur
Roars his mighty roar.
He wears no crown but he is king,
Ruler of them all.

He watches the playful cubs
Chasing butterflies
The insects manage to escape
And fly to the blue skies.

The females soon start to appear
Dragging the fine kill
He digs into the lovely meat
And eats up all his fill.

When the pride are fast asleep
Deep into the night
The king smells another male
He is ready to fight . . .

Katrina Blenkharn (9)
Kirkoswald CE Primary School

The Cat

A beast with eyes like sea blue crystals.
Fur as soft as a rug.
The teeth areas shiny as a pearl.
He slips away into the mist like a smoky ghost.

Callum Latimer (11)
Kirkoswald CE Primary School

Buzzing Bee

Buzzing bee to and fro
Flying high, flying low.
Working for its queen,
Can you guess it's a honeybee!
He is fast, look at him go,
Collecting nectar from the meadow.
Buzzing bee to and fro
Flying high, flying low.
Buzz, buzz, buzz!
Queen calling, got to go!

Hannah Frost (10)
Kirkoswald CE Primary School

George And The Dragon - Haikus

There was a dragon
Who lived in a big, dark cave.
He was so scary.

He was so hungry
A sheep was chosen to eat
And tied to a tree.

A new tasty meal.
They tied girls to a big tree.
Time for the princess.

Tied to a big tree,
She was shivering and scared.
The dragon had come.

She heard a clip-clop
George came with a spear, and so . . .
He killed the dragon.

Ellie Armstrong (10)
Kirkoswald CE Primary School

My Dog

My dog runs around the garden.
My dog sleeps in his bed.
My dog plays with other dogs.
My dog plays with me and he pulls the toy off me!

Calum Lennie (10)
Kirkoswald CE Primary School

Feelings

Anger is as red as a fire raging upon a poor helpless log.
Happiness is like a nice sunny summer's day.
Sadness is a horrible feeling, it is like you are continually digging a hole
and getting nowhere.
Joy is a great feeling, just as if you were a butterfly
flying silently through the sky.
Frustration is like you are crushed up in a small cage
in the corner of the room.
Stress is like you're tired, can't get motivated and can't be bothered.

Sam Borgogno (11)
Kirkoswald CE Primary School

Tip Tap

I can hear the chimes of the clock, one, two, three,
Tip, tap, tip, tap go the toes of tiny people
On the creaky floorboards of my room.
It's late at night and the air is heavy.
He has glistening eyes like dark midnight skies
And an old tattered hat of mouse leather.
He creeps around as light as a feather.
He has a cheeky grin and peculiar clothes,
Rather large ears and a cute button nose.
This is my little friend, his tale won't end
And this brownies name is Fimbletoe.

Connie Dalton (10)
Kirkoswald CE Primary School

My Bedroom

My wardrobe is like a door to Narnia.
When I open my drawers it is like a staircase to nowhere.
My lamp is like a sun shining through my window.
My CD player is like being at a party with people having fun.
My bedcover has words all over it, it is as if it is my friends
                                                    talking to me.

Lydia McGuiness (9)
Robert Ferguson Primary School

My Bedroom

My duvet is a blue wonderful sky.
My wardrobe is a stairway to Heaven.
My lamp is a mini moon.
My TV is a camera looking into my eyes.
My carpet is a sea, blue and calm.

Joshua Allen (8)
Robert Ferguson Primary School

My Bedroom

My bed is like a blue sparkling sea.
My wardrobe takes me to Narnia.
My carpet is warm to walk on and lie on.
My pencil case is warm like a woolly sheep.
My chest of drawers are like stairs.
My shoes can be a little car for a little doll.

Naomi Evans (8)
Robert Ferguson Primary School

Yellow

Yellow is the sun that gleams in the light.
Yellow is a sunflower sitting in a field.
Yellow is a star twinkling in the sky.
Yellow is my English book as I write a poem.
Yellow is the butter I spread on my bread.
Yellow is the bed covers I pull over me every night.
Yellow is the chicks that come out and live a life.

Alice McLean (9)
Robert Ferguson Primary School

My Bedroom

Inside my bedroom there is a wardrobe that is a den.
My bed is as comfortable as feathers from a hen.
Inside my bedroom my drawers are like stairs.
I tried to climb them and fell,
No one cares!

Ebony Harper (9)
Robert Ferguson Primary School

Blue

Blue is sky around the high sun.
Blue is the sea splashing against the walls.
Blue is bluebells growing each day.
Blue is the colour of someone's eyes staring at me.
Blue is my blue sweater top, all warm and fluffy.
Blue is a blue budgie in a big cage, tweeting and singing to me.

Becky Ward (8)
Robert Ferguson Primary School

Green

Green is grass growing in the gardens.
Green is a frog jumping near the pond.
Green is a round ball bouncing in the garden.
Green is a top hanging on the washing line.
Green is a bowl of jelly sitting on the table.
Green is a hat sitting on my head.
Green is a leaf falling from the trees.
Green is a traffic light that makes the cars go.
Green is a balloon floating in the air.
Green is a ruler for drawing straight lines.

Courtney Wood (8)
Robert Ferguson Primary School

Sandwiches

S ausage is a great treat
A pple is the healthy way to eat
N aughty is chocolates that put on the weight
D elightful are noodles which make you stay up late
W orrying is bacon from the greasy pan
I nsane is cheese and ketchup, I'm not a fan
C hips are really yummy in my tummy
H am is extremely scrummy, scrummy
E gg is very nice
S oup is full of spice.

Jade Selen (9)
Robert Ferguson Primary School

My Mum

My mum is as wonderful as can be,
She likes the colour blue like the stormy sea.
She always likes to read her book,
I always see her in luck.
She was impressed with my chair,
She likes the book, 'The Tortoise and the Hare'.
So that's my wonderful mum,
There's one thing you can't say,
Is that she buys too much chewing gum.

Thomas Chandler (9)
Robert Ferguson Primary School

Sandwiches

S ausage is scrummy, so sizzling hot
A pple is my best fruit, not!
N uts are so nasty to eat
D unkers are divine, such a treat
W alkers are wonderful to crunch so loud
I ce cream is insane, fluffy as a cloud
C risps are cheerful to crunch
H am is horrible for my lunch
E gg is lovely to eat
S alad is spectacular, especially in the heat.

Kelly Pearson (8)
Robert Ferguson Primary School

Yellow

Yellow is my box that gives light all night.
Yellow is my literacy book that's open all the time.
Yellow is a sunflower growing in the garden.
Yellow is my mum's hair that looks so shining all the time.
Yellow is my top that is so bright.
Yellow is my ball that is bouncing all the time.
Yellow is my stained-glass window that lights up every day.
Yellow is my pen and I use it every day.

Amy Stobbart (8)
Robert Ferguson Primary School

The Blue Poem

Blue is like berries, so sweet to eat.
Blue is like the ocean, as rough as it can be.
Blue is like the sky, as smooth as silk.
Blue is like a car zooming by.
Blue is the jumper we wear for school.

Luke Green (8)
Robert Ferguson Primary School

Yellow

Yellow is the sun, all bright and shiny.
Yellow is my hair, all short and clean.
Yellow is felt-tip pen that you colour with.
Yellow is a daffodil in the green grass.
Yellow is the Carlisle goalie top getting dirty in the mud.
Yellow is the literacy book I write my stories in.
Yellow is the traffic light setting people off.

Ben Clifford (9)
Robert Ferguson Primary School

Red

Red is the fire engine that goes rushing by that saves people.
Red is the cupboard next to the wall that people put stuff in.
Red is the old Carlisle strip that keeps the fans going.
Red is the blood that drips down, blood saves people's lives.
Red are the apples waiting to drop above the branches that are
waiting to snap.

Red is the paper that people use.

Ben Fenton (9)
Robert Ferguson Primary School

My Bedroom

My wardrobe is the door to Anfield as Liverpool fight for glory.
My television is an eye watching me as I watch it.
My bed is like a trampoline I jump on it to annoy my mum.
My lamp is like a little sun shining brightly in my light blue room.
My carpet is like the sand from a beach that reminds me
                                    of my holidays.
My dressing table is like wood from a chopped down tree.

Darcy Cannon (9)
Robert Ferguson Primary School

Yellow

Yellow is the colour of daffodils growing in the sun.
Yellow is the colour of the rising sun beaming on the water.
Yellow is the colour of my English book that I write in every day.
Yellow is the colour of our friction board as we learn in science.
Yellow is a banana as it ripens in the sun.
Yellow is a bee buzzing around a beehive.
Yellow is a flower that I grow at night.

Lucy Reay (8)
Robert Ferguson Primary School

My Bedroom

My carpet is the blue calm sea.
My TV is an eye, reading my mind as I sleep.
My mini football that I kick about every night, it's like a ball of lava.
My bed is a boat sailing on blue carpet.
My wardrobe leads me to my dreams
And my guitar is a castle of music.

Owen Moxon (9)
Robert Ferguson Primary School

Sandwiches

S is the softness of the wrapper
A is for appetising
N is for the nice tomatoes
D is delicious cheese and turkey
W is wonderful juicy tomatoes
I is the interesting taste
C is for the crunchiness of the lettuce
H is for the Hellmans squeezy cheese
E is for the elegance of the sauce
S is for the scrumptious wrap.

Carly Lloyd (9)
Robert Ferguson Primary School

The Red Poem

Red is an apple as sweet as can be.
Red is a tomato so juicy to me.
Red is a light that stops the cars.
Red is anger that can put people behind bars!

Steven McDowall (9)
Robert Ferguson Primary School

Sandwiches

S is scrummy sausages
A is an apple, gocd for you
N is nasty peas
D is dreadful potatoes
W is wonderful when you like something
 I is insane chocolate
C is chips dipped into tomato sauce
H is ham and cheese
E is egg, scrambled and fluffy
S is salad, lettuce, tomato and all.

Jake Riley (8)
Robert Ferguson Primary School

My Bedroom

My bedroom is lovely
I have a big bed so tall.
My bedroom is lovely
With a beautiful red wall.

My bedroom is lovely
With a warm carpet.
My bedroom is lovely
But the window is wet.

My bedroom is lovely
But can be such a mess.
My bedroom is lovely
When I've just tidied it, I guess.

James Graham (9)
Robert Ferguson Primary School

The Panther

I see a vicious panther
It prowls across the ground
To catch its prey.
Slowly, carefully, waiting to pounce.
Big with an extremely long tail,
Soft with a smooth head.
Roars loudly as it eats its prey.

Toby Theobald (9)
Robert Ferguson Primary School

Blue

Blue is the sea high and wavy.
Blue is a bluebell swaying in the breeze.
Blue is a raindrop falling from the sky.
Blue is the sky so very high.
Blue is a pen running out of ink.
Blue is some paint on our bedroom walls.

Oliver Saunders (8)
Robert Ferguson Primary School

My Bedroom

My bedroom, what a tip
When I see it I bite my lip.
It has clothes all over the floor,
I can't look at it when I open my door.
I have dusty shelves
I would love to have elves.
It has spiderwebs on the light,
I get scared at night.
My mum screams when she sees it,
She says, 'Tidy it bit by bit!'
Well, that's my room,
But now I'm going to get the vacuum.

Natalie Gorst (9)
Robert Ferguson Primary School

Green

Green is the vegetables all tasty and yummy.
Green is the grass, full of pretty flowers.
Green is the traffic light make sure you're good.
Green is the geography book full of different places.
Green is the tennis balls bounce, bounce everywhere.
Green is the traffic lights telling you to go.

Zoe Adams (8)
Robert Ferguson Primary School

Green

Green is as green as grass blowing in the wind.
Green is a leaf falling in the air.
Green is like an apple on the tree.
Green is a hairband sitting in her hair.

Kieran Thomas (8)
Robert Ferguson Primary School

The White Poem

White is the fluffy clouds floating across the sky.
White is the paper flying high.
White is the dog jumping up to welcome you.
White is the rabbit we mustn't eat in stew!

Taylor Millar (8)
Robert Ferguson Primary School

Sandwich

S crummy is the sandwich in my tummy
A pple sauce with pork is yummy
N asty is salami, a terrible taste
D readful is the chips, don't eat in haste
W onderful is some spaghetti like long legs
I nsane is worms and eggs
C hocolate is the loveliest thing around
H am is what you can buy by the pound
E ggs so soft and runny
S alad is the healthy thing so funny.

Chloe Strickland (8)
Robert Ferguson Primary School

Young Writers Information

We hope you have enjoyed reading this book - and that you will continue to enjoy it in the coming years.

If you like reading and writing poetry drop us a line, or give us a call, and we'll send you a free information pack.

Alternatively if you would like to order further copies of this book or any of our other titles, then please give us a call or log onto our website at www.youngwriters.co.uk

**Young Writers Information
Remus House
Coltsfoot Drive
Peterborough
PE2 9JX**

(01733) 890066